I·N·S·I·D·E
ISRAEL

Ian James

Franklin Watts
London · New York · Sydney · Toronto

CONTENTS

© 1990 Franklin Watts
96 Leonard Street
London EC2 4HA

Franklin Watts Inc.
387 Park Avenue South
New York, N.Y. 10016

Franklin Watts Australia
14 Mars Road
Lane Cove
NSW 2066

Design: K & Co
Illustrations: Hayward Art Group

UK ISBN: 0 7496 0063 2
US ISBN: 0-531-14028-8
Library of Congress Catalog
Card Number: 89-38985

Phototypeset by Lineage Ltd,
Watford

Printed in Belgium

Front cover: Sonia Halliday
Back cover: Hutchison Library
Frontispiece: Sonia Halliday
Photographs/Laura Lushington

Additional photographs: BIPAC 8B, 21;
Bridgeman Art Library/Dora
Holzhandler 22; Chris Fairclough 30;
Sonia Halliday Photographs 5T, 5B, 10,
11B, 23, 24B; Sonia Halliday
Photographs/Laura Lushington 4, 7, 13;
Sonia Halliday Photographs/Barrie
Searle 16T, 16B, 19, 20, 25, 27;
Hutchison Library 6, 11T, 24T, 26, 28,
29; Popperfoto 8T; Rex Features 9;
ZEFA 12, 15, 17, 18T, 18B.

The land

Israel, a small country in southwestern Asia, was created in 1948, but its history goes back thousands of years. In ancient times it was called Palestine, and it was here that two great religions, Judaism and Christianity, originated. Palestine is also a holy place to followers of Islam and it is often called the Holy Land. Because of its great religious importance, many pilgrims visit the country every year.

The main land regions, not including the occupied areas, are the Mediterranean coastal plains; hilly northern and central Israel; the Rift Valley, which contains the Sea of Galilee, the Jordan River and the Dead Sea; and the Negev desert in the south.

Below: **The Mediterranean Sea coast contains beautiful beaches and ancient settlements, such as the port of Acre just north of Haifa.**

Above: **The Dead Sea is the saltiest body of water in the world. It lies in a deep rift valley on Israel's border with Jordan.**

Left: **The River Jordan flows from the Sea of Galilee into the Dead Sea.**

The Mediterranean coastal plains are densely populated. Inland, lie the fertile Galilean Highlands in the north and the Judean Hills in central Israel. The country's highest point, excluding the occupied areas, is Mount Meron in the Galilean Highlands.

The Rift Valley is part of a huge break in the Earth's crust. The most fertile part of the valley lies north of the freshwater Sea of Galilee, which is fed by the Jordan River. The river then flows south into the salty Dead Sea. The Dead Sea shoreline is about 400 m (1,312 ft) below sea level. This is the world's lowest point on land. The Negev Desert extends south to the port of Eilat on the Gulf of Aqaba, an arm of the Red Sea. Israel has hot, dry summers. Winters are mild and rainy in the north. The south is dry.

Above: **The Negev Desert in southern Israel is the country's driest region.**

The people and their history

Israel was created in 1948 as a home for Jews. Today, more than four-fifths of the people are Jewish; many are immigrants. Most of the others are Arabs. Many languages are spoken in Israel, but the two official languages are Hebrew and Arabic.

A people called Hebrews, who were later called Jews, settled in Palestine in about 1900 BC. The area was conquered many times. In the 2nd century AD, after a revolt against the Romans, many Jews were driven out of Palestine in what is called the Diaspora, or the "scattering". Over the centuries that followed, Jews prayed that they would return one day.

Below: **The fortress at Masada, overlooking the Dead Sea, was the scene of the last stand of Jewish patriots against Roman rule in AD 73. The patriots committed suicide instead of surrendering.**

Left: **After World War II, many European Jews went to Palestine, hoping that one day it would become an independent Jewish state.**

Below: **David Ben-Gurion proclaimed Israel's independence on May 14, 1948.**

Many Palestinians became Muslims after the Arabs occupied the area in the 7th century. From the late 19th century, European Jews began to settle in Palestine, which was then ruled by Turkey. Some Jews, called Zionists, wanted to make Palestine a Jewish state, but most Arabs opposed this policy.

In 1947, the United Nations voted to split Palestine into a Jewish and an Arab state. The Jewish state of Israel was proclaimed on May 14, 1948. Troops from six Arab countries invaded Israel. War raged until a ceasefire was agreed in July 1949. Fighting has occurred several times since 1949, and Israel has gained land from Egypt, Jordan and Syria.

Below: **Former President Jimmy Carter applauds the Israeli Prime Minister Menachim Begin and the Egyptian President Anwar el Sadat who signed a peace treaty between their countries in 1979.**

Towns and cities

Some Israelis live in farming communities and many Arabs live in farming villages. However, nine out of every ten people live in towns or cities. The largest city is Jerusalem, followed by Tel Aviv-Jaffa and Haifa.

Tel Aviv-Jaffa once consisted of two cities, Tel Aviv and Jaffa (or Yafo in Hebrew), which were combined in 1950. Today, it is Israel's leading commercial and industrial city. Jaffa is an ancient port, important in biblical times, while Tel Aviv was founded in 1909 by Jewish immigrants from Europe. Haifa, which is north of Tel Aviv, is Israel's main port. It has many industries including oil and chemicals.

Below: **Tel Aviv is a modern city, with tall buildings overlooking the sea.**

Above: **Haifa became important in the 1850s when its port was developed.**

Left: **The Church of the Annunciation in the town of Nazareth in northern Israel is an important Christian shrine.**

11

Israel has many places of historic interest. Nazareth, capital of the Northern district, was the town where Jesus spent his boyhood. It has many religious sites.

Beersheba, capital of the Southern district, is said to be the place where Abraham, father of the Hebrew people, settled. Abraham's traditional burial place is Hebron, which is in the Israeli-occupied West Bank. Near Hebron is Bethlehem, birthplace of Jesus. The ancient port of Acre (or 'Akko), north of Haifa, has ruins associated with the Crusades. The port of Eilat (or Elat), in the far south on the Gulf of Aqaba, is an important seaside resort.

Below: **Beersheba is the capital of the Negev, a desert region in southern Israel.**

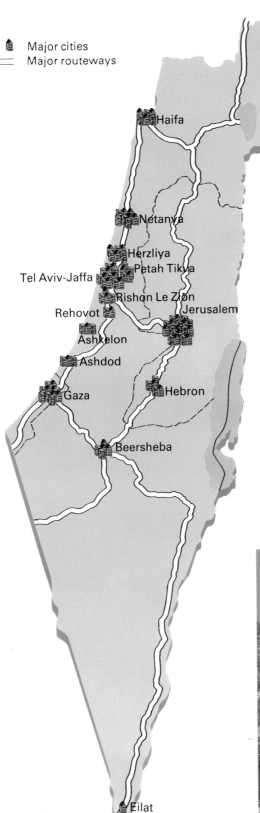

Major cities
Major routeways

Haifa

Netanya

Herzliya
Petah Tikva
Tel Aviv-Jaffa
Rishon Le Zion
Rehovot
Jerusalem
Ashkelon
Ashdod
Gaza
Hebron

Beersheba

Eilat

Left: **The map shows major routes and cities in Israel.**

Below: **The Dome of the Rock in Jerusalem is sacred to Muslims. It stands on a rock where Muslims believe Muhammad rose to heaven.**

Christians, Jews and Muslims all regard Jerusalem as a holy city. It became capital of the united Israelite tribes under King David in about 1000 BC. The Israelis have made it their capital. But many countries refused to recognize this act because of a United Nations plan to make it an international city.

In 1948, West Jerusalem was held by Israel, and East Jerusalem by Jordan. But in 1967, Israel occupied the East. They gained the Western (or Wailing) Wall — a remnant of the Jews' holy temple destroyed by the Romans in AD 70 — the Church of the Holy Sepulchre on the hill of Calvary where Jesus died and the Muslim Dome of the Rock.

Below: **The map shows some of the landmarks of Jerusalem.**

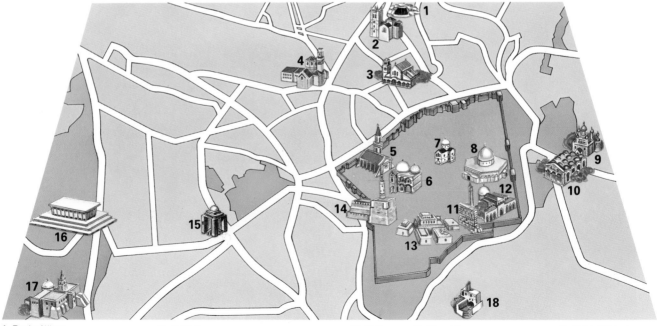

1. Tomb of Kings	**5.** St. Savior	**10.** Gethsemane Basilica of Agony	**15.** Heichal Shlomo
2. St. George Cathedral	**6.** Church of the Holy Sepulchre	**11.** Hakotel Hammaravi (Western Wall)	**16.** Knesset
3. St. Stephen's Basilica	**7.** Armenian Cathedral Patriarchate	**12.** El Aqsa Mosque	**17.** Monastery of the Cross
4. Italian Hospital	**8.** Dome of the Rock	**13.** Yeshivat Porat Yosef	**18.** Pool of Siloam
	9. St. Mary Magdalen	**14.** David's Tower	

Family life

Most Israelis live in comfortable but small apartments. They have higher standards of living than many people in southwestern Asia. Most families have a television set, but many people prefer to spend their time meeting friends, playing games, or singing.

In collective communities called kibbutzim (kibbutzim is the plural of kibbutz), people receive services, including housing, food and medical care, instead of wages. Adults eat together in a dining hall, while the children usually live in a children's community. Parents see their children after work, on the Sabbath (the Jewish holy day, lasting from sunset on Friday to sunset on Saturday), and during festivals.

Below: **The people who live on kibbutzim eat together in large dining halls. But they have separate living areas.**

Above: **Reading is a popular pastime in Israel.**

Left: **Many of the Arabs who live in Israel wear traditional clothes.**

Food

Many Israelis follow kashrut, the dietary law of Judaism. Their food must be kosher, which means "ritually correct". Orthodox Jews do not eat pork or shellfish. Meat and milk products may not be eaten at the same meal.

Because Israelis have come from so many countries, most towns have a wide range of international restaurants, in addition to Arab and Jewish ones. Lots of vegetables and fruit are eaten, and chicken and turkey are popular meats. One famous dish is *falafel.* It consists of fried balls of chick peas or white beans mixed with onions, garlic and spices. *Falafel* are usually served in pockets of flat bread and sold from stalls in the street.

Below: **Fresh vegetables are sold at this market in the Old City of Jerusalem.**

Left: **Snacks are prepared at stalls in the streets.**

Below: **The matza (unleavened bread) is blessed at the annual feast of the Passover. This feast commemorates the exodus of the Israelites from captivity in Egypt.**

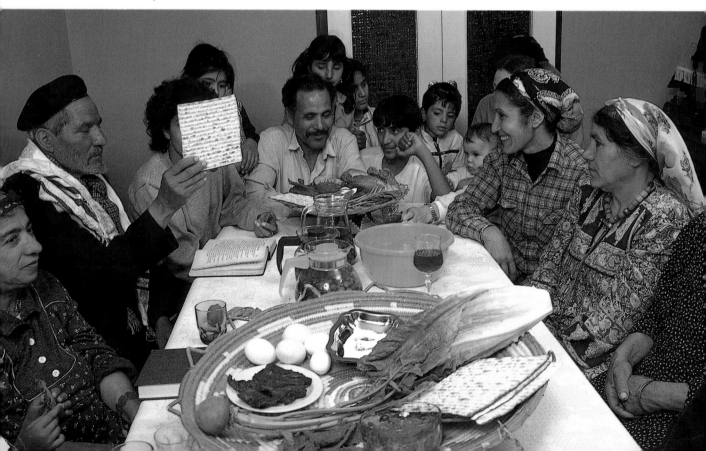

Sports and pastimes

Above: **Soccer is a popular team game in Israel.**

Both schools and the armed forces place a strong emphasis on physical fitness. Although Israelis work a six-day week, they play a wide range of games and sports. Badminton, basketball and chess are sports at which Israelis have been especially successful. Soccer is another popular team game, and many people take part in gymnastics, tennis and golf. Most people live near the sea and enjoy a variety of water sports.

The Maccabiah Games, which are held in Israel, are similar to the Olympic Games. They have been held once every four years since 1932. The Maccabiah Games attract Jewish athletes from all over the world.

19

Watching television, listening to the radio, and reading books and newspapers are leading pastimes. This is partly because most Israelis are very interested in news about their country and the surrounding Arab world. Israel has newspapers in the two official languages, Hebrew and Arabic, and in other languages, including Yiddish, a European dialect spoken by millions of Jews around the world.

Music and dance are other important pastimes. Many young people enjoy disco music, as well as folk dances and folksongs rooted in Jewish culture. Oriental Jews (Jews from Asian or North African countries) and Arabs also have their own traditional music and dances.

Above: **Many people enjoy swimming in the warm Mediterranean Sea.**

The arts

Israel is a young country and its national arts are still developing. But Jewish culture and the Hebrew language go back thousands of years. Among modern writers in Hebrew is Shmuel Yosef Agnon (1888-1970), who won the 1966 Nobel prize for literature. Israel has several distinguished drama companies, including the national company, Habima, meaning The Stage. It has its own building in Tel Aviv, but it performs all over the country. Israel also has a lively motion picture industry.

Music is one of the most important art forms. Israel has six major orchestras, including the famous Israel Philharmonic Orchestra which was founded in 1936. The country has also produced many great soloists.

Below: **The Israel Philharmonic Orchestra has an international reputation. Its conductor, in this picture, is Daniel Barenboim.**

Ballet is a very popular musical art and Israel has some fine dance companies. A new and distinctive style has emerged which combines classical ballet with traditional Middle Eastern dance.

Painting and sculpture are largely influenced by European work, but local Israeli schools of painters have emerged. The country has many museums that preserve Jewish art. Others display archaeological remains and help people to understand the history of Jews around the world. The Shrine of the Book, in Jerusalem, houses the Dead Sea scrolls, which include the oldest known manuscripts of the Old Testament.

Below: **Much Israeli art celebrates Jewish traditions. This painting, called "The Passover Meal", is by the Israeli artist Dora Holzhandler.**

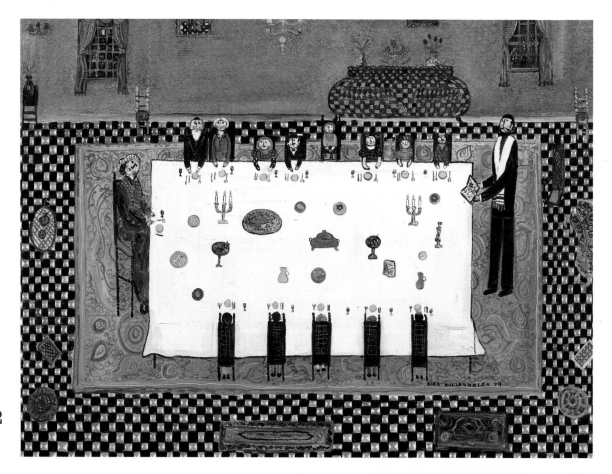

Farming

Farming employs about six percent of Israel's workers. But only about one-fifth of the land is used for crops. Much of it is irrigated. Wheat and fruit, especially oranges, are the leading crops. Cotton, olives, eggs, milk and poultry are also important, but Israel has to import about two-fifths of the food it needs.

Some farms are privately owned. But many farms are based on the kibbutz or moshav systems. On a kibbutz, people work together and share the earnings of their community. On a moshav, each family farms its own land, but the village provides equipment and supplies, and markets the produce.

Below: **Much of Israel lacks enough rain for farming. Most of the land is irrigated. The water is brought by pipeline from other areas.**

Right: **Oranges and other citrus fruits are major crops in Israel.**

Below: **Beef cattle graze on rough pasture in northern and central Israel.**

Industry

Israel has few natural resources. Bromine and potash, which are used in the chemical industry, are mined near the Dead Sea. Phosphate rock, which is used to make fertilizers, is mined in the Negev Desert. Some copper and magnesium are also mined, but most other minerals used in industry have to be imported.

More than half of the country's factories are located in or near the city of Tel Aviv-Jaffa. Major industries include the refining of imported oil and the manufacture of aircraft and aerospace equipment, chemicals, construction materials, electrical goods, machinery, metals and plastics. Other important activities are food processing and the cutting of imported diamonds.

Below: **Potash, important to Israel's chemical industry, is mined in the Dead Sea area.**

25

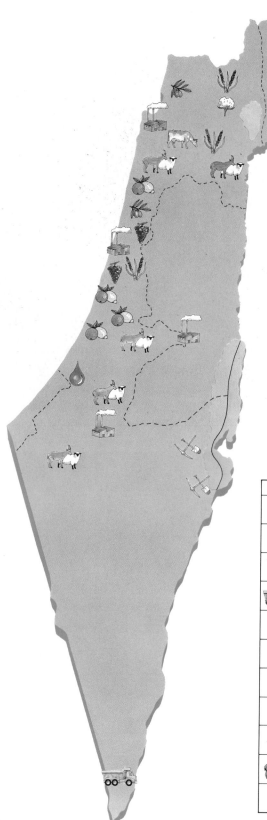

Below: **Oil is imported to fuel electricity generating plants.**

Left: **The map shows some of the economic activities in Israel.**

Key:	
	Industry
	Petroleum
	Potash, bromine and magnesium
	Copper
	Citrus fruits
	Olives
	Cereals
	Cotton
	Sheep and goats
	Grapes

Israel's economic success owes much to its scientists. They have made great contributions in the fields of electronics, nuclear power, and the production of computer hardware and software. Israel has also developed its own arms industry and manufactures jet aircraft. The lack of fuels has led to much research in the field of alternative energy, especially the harnessing of solar power. Israel has sent scientists to developing countries to help them improve their agricultural and industrial methods.

Foreign trade is important to Israel. Its main trading partners are the countries of Western Europe and the United States.

Above: **The manufacture of gold rings and diamond cutting are major industries in Israel.**

Looking to the future

Israel has had to fight to survive. Wars with Arab forces occurred in 1948-49, 1956, 1967 and 1973. During these wars, Israel occupied several areas, including the Sinai Peninsula. But, under a peace treaty agreed in 1978, Israel returned this desert region to Egypt between 1979 and 1982. This treaty gave rise to hopes of peace. But Israel still controls three other occupied areas: the Gaza Strip on the Mediterranean Sea coast; the West Bank, an area west of the Dead Sea and Jordan River; and the Golan Heights in the northeast.

Protests by Arabs against the Israeli occupation of these three areas have led to much violence.

Below: **The army plays an important part in preserving the state of Israel. Military service of 3 years for all Jewish men and 2 years for all unmarried women is compulsory.**

Left: **Many young people, Jews and Arabs alike, hope that one day Israel will be able to live in peace with all Arab countries.**

Much opposition to Israel has come from the Palestine Liberation Organization (PLO), which represents Palestinian Arabs, who want their own state. The PLO has attacked Israel and, in return, Israel attacked PLO military bases in Lebanon. In December 1988, Yasir Arafat, the PLO chairman, recognized Israel's right to exist. He denounced terrorist actions against Israel.

Facts about Israel

Area:
22,770 sq km (8,019 sq miles) The figure does not include any of the disputed occupied territories

Population:
4,512,000

Capital: Jerusalem

Largest cities:
Jerusalem (483,000)
Tel Aviv-Jaffa (319,000)
Haifa (223,000)

Official languages:
Hebrew, Arabic

Religions:
In 1986, Jews 3,561,000, Muslims 586,000, Christians 100,000, Druzes and others 73,000

Main exports:
Manufactured goods, machinery and transportation equipment, diamonds

Unit of currrency:
Shekel

Israel compared with other countries

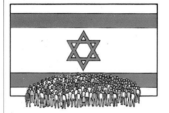

Israel 217 per sq km

Britain 232 per sq km

USA 26 per sq km

Australia 2 per sq km

Above: **How many people?** Israel is, on average, a fairly densely populated country.

Below: **How large? Israel is only about one-tenth the size of the United Kingdom.**

USA

Australia

UK   Israel

Below: **Some money and stamps used in Israel.**

LEBANON

Golan Heights
Under Israeli Occupation

SYRIA

1,208m ▲
Mount Meron

Zefat

*Sea of
Galilee*

Haifa

Tiberia

Nazareth

MEDITERRANEAN SEA

Afula

Hadera

Jenin

Jordan River

Tulkarm

Sarqa River

Narlus

Petah Tikva

Tel Aviv

West Bank
Under Israeli
Occupation

Ramla

Jericho

Jerusalem

Ashquelon

Bethlehem

Gaza Strip
Under Israeli Occupation

Gaza

Hebron

*Dead
Sea*

Rafam

JORDAN

Beersheba

ISRAEL

Negev Desert

EGYPT

Scale 1:1,100,00

0   10   20   30 miles

0   10   20   30   40   50 km

Eilat

Index